Yak in the Back

Islamic Reader
Level 2

By
Karemah Alhark
And
Jamila Alqarnain

Illustrated By
Khadijah Amatur-Raheem
Najla Amatur-Raheem
and
Jamila Alqarnain

Noon
PUBLICATIONS

Islamic Phonics Readers

THIS IS AN ISLAMIC CHILDREN'S READER PUBLISHED BY
NOON PUBLICATIONS

Say:
Surely my prayer
and my sacrifice
and my life
and my death
are (all) for Allah,
the Lord of the worlds.
(The Cattle: 6.162)

Dear Educators,

Asalamu Alaykum and Greetings!

We are very pleased to present the second book in our series of seven Islamic phonics readers: **Yak in the Back**. As with all of our phonics based books, this volume is filled with fun and colorful pages designed to teach children reading proficiency.

Yak in the Back focuses on the short vowel sounds "a, e, i, o and u". In addition to regularly reading this book with your young learner(s), please use our **Level 2 Phonics Flashcards** for additional daily practice. With this reader you will teach your student(s) how to sound out and blend (combine) sounds to form words. It is very important to be consistent and make it fun. This practice will better prepare children for mastering all of the readers in this series.

Our texts not only provide the skills to become a successful reader, they are also filled with beautifully illustrated, diverse characters and stories that teach ethics. This is important in developing a positive self-image and becoming familiar with Islamic morals and principles.

We are dedicated to the task of creating quality, Islamic curriculum for Muslim children. As we continue to serve the Ummah, we pray that our work will be well received. It is our sincere hope that these readers will be the gateway to literacy for many young learners.

Sincerely,

The Noon Publications Team

Vocabulary - Short "a"

Dad	gas
van	fast
fam	can
yak	pass
back	hat
map	

Sight Words

a	with
the	and
is	he's
in	has
on	

Yak in the Back

Dad has a van.

The fam is in the van.

The yak is in the back!

Dad has the map.

Gas is in the van.

The van is fast.

The van can pass.

The yak has a hat and
he's on Dad's back!

The van is back with
the fam and the yak.

Vocabulary - Short "e"

Jen's	peck
Jen	wet
hens	mess
beg	pet
get	pep
gets	led
fed	bed

Sight Words

they	what
go	new
to	

Jen's Hens

Jen has hens.

The hens beg.

The hens get fed.

The hens peck.

The hens get wet.

What a wet mess!

Jen has a new pet.

The pet has pep.

The pet gets wet.

What a wet mess!

The hens get led.

The pet gets led.

The hens and the pet rest.

Vocabulary - Short "i"

Ihsan	kick
this	lick
hill	mix
will	hit
visit	kiss
mill	

Sight Words

ma	Ihsan
his	

Ihsan

This is Ihsan.

Ihsan will kick.

Ihsan will lick.

Ihsan will mix.

Ihsan will visit a mill.

Ihsan will hit.

Ihsan will kiss his ma.

Vocabulary - Short "o"

Pop	rod
tots	cod
pond	how
box	odd
hop	God
jog	gobs
log	

Sight Words

no	are

Pop and Tots

Pop and tots are at a pond.

The tots hop.

The tots jog on a log.

Pop has a rod.

Pop gets no cod.

No cod? How odd!
The tots and Pop ask God.

Pop gets cod.

Gobs and gobs and gobs of cod!

Vocabulary - Short "u"

bugs	bees
jump	buzz
run	fuzz
sit	bud
bun	rub
hunt	mug

Sight Words

have	my

Bugs

Bugs jump.

Bugs run!

Bugs hunt.

Bugs have fuzz.

Bees buzz.

But bees are not bugs.

Bugs on buds.

Bugs rub.

Bugs in my mug?!

Made in the USA
Columbia, SC
12 September 2022